D1021970

To Alison McLean

LEO

A guide to living your best astrological life

STELLA ANDROMEDA

ILLUSTRATED BY EVI O. STUDIO

Hardie Grant

BOOKS

III.
Give Me More

Introduction

Inscribed on the forecourt of the ancient Greek temple of Apollo at Delphi are the words 'know thyself'. This is one of the 147 Delphic maxims, or rules to live by, attributed to Apollo himself, and was later extended by the philosopher Socrates to the sentence, 'The unexamined life is not worth living.'

People seek a variety of ways of knowing themselves, of coming to terms with life and trying to find ways to understand the challenges of human existence, often through therapy or belief systems like organised religion. These are ways in which we strive to understand the relationships we have with ourselves and others better, seeking out particular tools that enable us to do so.

As far as systems of understanding human nature and experience go, astrology has much to offer through its symbolic use of the constellations of the heavens, the depictions of the zodiac signs, the planets and their energetic effects. Many people find accessing this information and harnessing its potential a useful way of thinking about how to manage their lives more effectively.

What is astrology?

In simple terms, astrology is the study and interpretation of how the planets can influence us, and the world in which we live, through an understanding of their positions at a specific place in time. The practice of astrology relies on a combination of factual knowledge of the characteristics of these positions and their psychological interpretation.

Astrology is less of a belief system and more of a tool for living, from which ancient and established wisdom can be drawn. Any of us can learn to use astrology, not so much for divination or telling the future, but as a guidebook that provides greater insight and a more thoughtful way of approaching life. Timing is very much at the heart of astrology, and knowledge of planetary configurations and their relationship to each other at specific moments in time can assist in helping us with the timing of some of our life choices and decisions.

Knowing when major life shifts can occur – because of particular planetary configurations such as a Saturn return (see page 103) or Mercury retrograde (see page 104) – or what it means to have Venus in your seventh house (see pages 85 and 98), while recognising the specific characteristics of your sign, are all tools that you can use to your advantage. Knowledge is power, and astrology can be a very powerful supplement to approaching life's ups and downs and any relationships we form along the way.

The 12 signs of the zodiac

Each sign of the zodiac has a range of recognisable characteristics, shared by people born under that sign. This is your Sun sign, which you probably already know – and the usual starting point from which we each begin to explore our own astrological paths. Sun sign characteristics can be strongly exhibited in an individual's make-up; however, this is only part of the picture.

Usually, how we appear to others is tempered by the influence of other factors – and these are worth bearing in mind. Your ascendant sign is equally important, as is the positioning of your Moon. You can also look to your opposite sign to see what your Sun sign may need a little more of, to balance its characteristics.

After getting to know your Sun sign in the first part of this book, you might want to dive into the Give Me More section (see pages 74–105) to start to explore all the particulars of your birth chart. These will give you far greater insight into the myriad astrological influences that may play out in your life.

Sun signs

It takes 365 (and a quarter, to be precise) days for the Earth to orbit the Sun and in so doing, the Sun appears to us to spend a month travelling through each sign of the zodiac. Your Sun sign is therefore an indication of the sign that the Sun was travelling through at the time of your birth. Knowing what Sun signs you and your family, friends and lovers are provides you with just the beginning of the insights into character and personality that astrology can help you discover.

On the cusp

For those for whom a birthday falls close to the end of one Sun sign and the beginning of another, it's worth knowing what time you were born. There's no such thing, astrologically, as being 'on the cusp' – because the signs begin at a specific time on a specific date, although this can vary a little year on year. If you are not sure, you'll need to know your birth date, birth time and birth place to work out accurately to which Sun sign you belong. Once you have these, you can consult an astrologer or run your details through an online astrology site program (see page 108) to give you the most accurate birth chart possible.

Taurus

The bull

21 APRIL–20 MAY

Grounded, sensual and appreciative of bodily pleasures, Taurus is a fixed earth sign endowed by its ruling planet Venus with grace and a love of beauty, despite its depiction as a bull. Generally characterised by an easy and uncomplicated, if occasionally stubborn, approach to life, Taurus' opposite sign is watery Scorpio.

Aries

The ram

21 MARCH–20 APRIL

Astrologically the first sign of the zodiac, Aries appears alongside the vernal (or spring) equinox. A cardinal fire sign, depicted by the ram, it is the sign of beginnings and ruled by planet Mars, which represents a dynamic ability to meet challenges energetically and creatively. Its opposite sign is airy Libra.

Gemini

The twins

★

21 MAY–20 JUNE

A mutable air sign symbolised by the twins, Gemini tends to see both sides of an argument, its speedy intellect influenced by its ruling planet Mercury. Tending to fight shy of commitment, this sign also epitomises a certain youthfulness of attitude. Its opposite sign is fiery Sagittarius.

Cancer

The crab

★

21 JUNE–21 JULY

Depicted by the crab and the tenacity of its claws, Cancer is a cardinal water sign, emotional and intuitive, its sensitivity protected by its shell. Ruled by the maternal Moon, the shell also represents the security of home, to which Cancer is committed. Its opposite sign is earthy Capricorn.

Leo

The lion

★

22 JULY–21 AUGUST

A fixed fire sign, ruled by the Sun, Leo loves to shine and is an idealist at heart, positive and generous to a fault. Depicted by the lion, Leo can roar with pride and be confident and uncompromising, with a great faith and trust in humanity. Its opposite sign is airy Aquarius.

Virgo

The virgin

★

22 AUGUST–21 SEPTEMBER

Traditionally represented as a maiden or virgin, this mutable earth sign is observant, detail oriented and tends towards self-sufficiency. Ruled by Mercury, Virgos benefit from a sharp intellect that can be self-critical, while often being very health conscious. Its opposite sign is watery Pisces.

Scorpio

The scorpion

22 OCTOBER–21 NOVEMBER

Given to intense feelings, as
befits a fixed water sign, Scorpio
is depicted by the scorpion – linking
it to the rebirth that follows death –
and is ruled by both Pluto and Mars.
With a strong spirituality and deep
emotions, Scorpio needs security to
transform its strength. Its opposite
sign is earthy Taurus.

Libra

The scales

22 SEPTEMBER–21 OCTOBER

A cardinal air sign, ruled by Venus,
Libra is all about beauty, balance
(as depicted by the scales) and
harmony in its rather romanticised,
ideal world. With a strong aesthetic
sense, Libra can be both arty and
crafty, but also likes fairness and
can be very diplomatic. Its
opposite sign is fiery Aries.

Sagittarius

The archer

★

22 NOVEMBER–21 DECEMBER

Depicted by the archer, Sagittarius is a mutable fire sign that's all about travel and adventure, in body or mind, and is very direct in approach. Ruled by the benevolent Jupiter, Sagittarius is optimistic with lots of ideas; liking a free rein, but with a tendency to generalise. Its opposite sign is airy Gemini.

Capricorn

The goat

★

22 DECEMBER–20 JANUARY

Ruled by Saturn, Capricorn is a cardinal earth sign associated with hard work and depicted by the sure-footed and sometimes playful goat. Trustworthy and unafraid of commitment, Capricorn is often very self-sufficient and has the discipline for the freelance working life. Its opposite sign is the watery Cancer.

Aquarius
The water carrier

★

21 JANUARY–19 FEBRUARY

Confusingly, given its depiction
by the water carrier, Aquarius
is a fixed air sign ruled by the
unpredictable Uranus, sweeping
away old ideas with innovative
thinking. Tolerant, open-minded
and all about humanity, its vision
is social with a conscience. Its
opposite sign is fiery Leo.

Pisces
The fish

★

20 FEBRUARY–20 MARCH

Acutely responsive to its
surroundings, Pisces is a mutable
water sign depicted by two fish,
swimming in opposite directions,
sometimes confusing fantasy with
reality. Ruled by Neptune, its
world is fluid, imaginative and
empathetic, often picking up on
the moods of others. Its opposite
sign is earthy Virgo.

Know

Leo

The sign the Sun
was travelling in at the
time you were born is the
ultimate starting point
in exploring your character
and personality through
the zodiac.

Fixed fire sign,
depicted by the lion.

Ruled by the Sun, the primary
life-giving force in the zodiac,
and representative of where
we all come from.

OPPOSITE SIGN

Aquarius

STATEMENT OF SELF

'I will.'

Lucky colour

The colours of the Sun in full beam, shining onto the world – orange and regal gold (of course). Wear these colours and connect with your Leo energy when you need a psychological boost and additional courage, choosing accessories – shoes, gloves, socks, hat or even underwear – if you don't have other clothes in this colour.

Lucky day

Sunday, literally Sun-day, and derived from the old Anglo-Saxon for *Sunnandæg* which became the day for worship of the life-giving Sun, the provider of light and life, named *Helios* by the Greeks and *Apollo* by the Romans.

Lucky gem

Considered the gem of kings, the powerful red ruby is
Leo's stone, thought to have the ability to restore vitality
and vigour, to be a potent aphrodisiac, and symbolic of the
dynamism of life and the powerful feelings it can evoke.

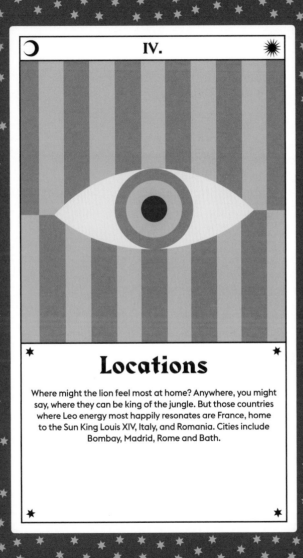

Locations

Where might the lion feel most at home? Anywhere, you might say, where they can be king of the jungle. But those countries where Leo energy most happily resonates are France, home to the Sun King Louis XIV, Italy, and Romania. Cities include Bombay, Madrid, Rome and Bath.

Holidays

Sun worship has to feature for Leo on holiday, but their adventurous spirit also means they want intellectual stimulation and possibly luxury, too, so a mere beach holiday won't always cut it. Rome, Prague and Hollywood all fit the bill, flying first-class of course.

Flowers

Leo's flower is the sunflower, depicting as it does the golden face of the Sun. In ancient myth, the nymph Clytie was turned into a sunflower, after gazing in unrequited love at the Sun god Apollo. In French it is known as *tournesol*, which literally means, to turn towards the Sun.

VII.

Trees

Citrus trees, bearing the highly prized and much treasured 'golden fruits' of oranges or lemons, are those associated with the sign ruled by the Sun. In ancient Greek and Roman mythology, citrus fruits were the dowry of Hera (Juno), the bride of Zeus (Jupiter).

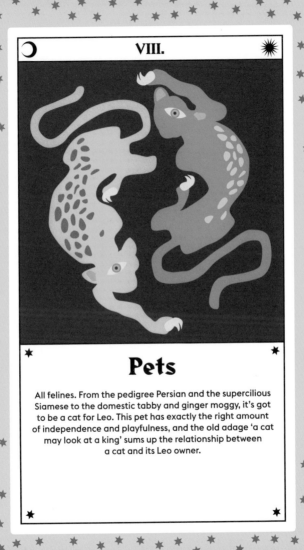

Pets

All felines. From the pedigree Persian and the supercilious Siamese to the domestic tabby and ginger moggy, it's got to be a cat for Leo. This pet has exactly the right amount of independence and playfulness, and the old adage 'a cat may look at a king' sums up the relationship between a cat and its Leo owner.

Parties

Basically, any party that treats them like royalty is Leo's style.
They like to make an entrance and lord it up, taking to the dance
floor like a pro and behaving like the host even when they're not.
Their natural *joie de vivre* mean they are welcome guests,
and will often show up with a crate of wine or magnum
of champagne, ensuring the mood is bright and fun.

Leo
characteristics

Leo is often immediately obvious, even from the other side of the room, and certainly once they've opened their mouths to speak. They tend to have a larger-than-life personality and actively enjoy being noticed and admired, adored and appreciated, often deliberately working to engage the attention of the crowd to achieve this. Leo is almost never a shrinking violet or a wall flower; but mixed with this exuberant and outgoing approach is a very real affection and loyalty for their family and friends. There's not much they won't do for those they love and they are generous with their time and gifts.

Ruled by the Sun, Leo also likes to shine on their world whether it's large or small, radiating energy and exuding cheerfulness like a sunny day. That energy often makes them strongly creative, whether in artistic or business endeavours, and even with an eye to their own legacy, sometimes to the extent of wanting to be immortalised in some way through their creation of something of lasting value. If you hear a man or woman being dubbed as being a 'golden boy' or girl, or of living a 'gilded life' then chances are they're a Leo.

Leo is also an idealist with a strong, almost child-like inner vision, and a self-belief that's difficult to thwart. Even if circumstances challenge it, they believe things will go well and will make them so, as they believe in their own positive destiny. It's partly this that makes them successful, although the downside of such conviction can sometimes blind them to how badly they are behaving in order to get things their own way. For the leader of the pack, being a team player isn't always a priority, which can be their undoing, as pride often comes before a fall from grace. If they do trip up, after making a bit of a song and dance about it, Leo tends to lick their wounds, pick themselves up, dust themselves down and start all over again: lesson learned.

Leo's extroverted nature makes them the life and soul of the party, and they will go to some lengths to embrace the theatrical and the dramatic. This can sometimes translate into everyday life as attention seeking and showing off, which are the less attractive features of Leo. Also, pride might be a feature – like the proud lion – a characteristic which can lead Leo to behave like their own worst enemy. Luckily, their sunny nature often compensates for these occasional failings, and they are quick to make amends.

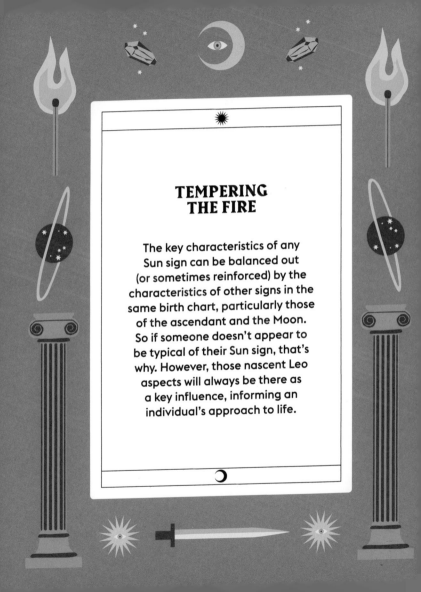

TEMPERING THE FIRE

The key characteristics of any Sun sign can be balanced out (or sometimes reinforced) by the characteristics of other signs in the same birth chart, particularly those of the ascendant and the Moon. So if someone doesn't appear to be typical of their Sun sign, that's why. However, those nascent Leo aspects will always be there as a key influence, informing an individual's approach to life.

Physical Leo

Even if a Leo is physically petite, there's something larger than life about them, and their physical presence is often so bold and outgoing in appearance or dress, that they give the impression of taking up more space than they actually do. This may be because they have lots of flowing, leonine hair, expansive gestures or a loud and flamboyant manner of speaking. Often Leo imagines they're playing a part, so their appearance reflects this and for them, appearance is pretty important and they will spend considerable time achieving the look they want the world to see.

Health

The back can be susceptible in Leo, often because they tend to roar around, over-exerting themselves generally and aren't great about taking the regular exercise necessary to keep muscles strong to support the spine. For the same reasons, the heart is also susceptible, and stress too can cause problems here along with any over-indulgence in food and alcohol. Leo tends to go at things head on and then fall over in a deflated heap. Luckily, an underlying robustness means they quickly recover, but Leo seldom seems to learn to pace themselves so there's a tendency for it to happen over and over again.

Exercise

If anyone has a personal trainer, it's likely to be Leo, who likes the attention even as they're being put through their paces. The social aspect of a gym is attractive to Leo, too and provides them with something of an audience to show off their prowess. But there's no guarantee Leo will turn up regularly to class; there may be something *much* more interesting going on elsewhere.

How Leo
communicates

I am Leo, hear me roar! And you will hear them, often before you see them, because this is often how Leo attracts the attention they seek. There can be a flamboyance about the way Leo speaks, a born raconteur who knows how to deliver, and with drama to hold their audience's attention. And that's part of it for Leo, who communicates to and for an audience, even if that's an audience of one. It is important to Leo, too, that what they say is considered worth saying – whether this is expressing a political view or gossiping about last night's TV – it has to be worth it, because this validates them. This need to be validated can make them quite challenging in an argument – a position you will often find them in as they love to debate (and, it has to be said, like the sound of their own voice!).

Leo careers

As might be expected, Leo is a natural performer, so acting, singing or dancing may be an expression of both their creativity and their desire for an audience. Whatever they do, they tend to work hard at it and make a success of it, even if they may switch careers over the course of a lifetime. That ability to perform can also take them into other public-facing careers like teaching, where Leo loves to share their wisdom to a younger generation and mentor the brightest minds. Or into law, corporate hospitality or public relations.

They also have a talent for entrepreneurship, happy to see the big picture and work hard to realise a creative dream, so the tech industry might beckon too. That same boldness and clarity of vision can make Leo an excellent leader, and they have the charisma to inspire others, making them a very effective company CEO. That vision can also take them the other side of the movie camera, not performing but directing the performers, where the Leo ability to tell stories can be written on a large canvas, communicated to many.

How Leo chimes

There is a bit of a tendency with Leo to choose partners that enhance them in some way. Someone who will reflect their light, amplify their qualities and provide them with an adoring audience. For love to chime, this slightly child-like approach to relationships needs to be tempered with a little consideration and objectivity; and a commitment to their partner and their wishes, dreams and needs, too. True, Leo demands a lot of attention, but it would be a big mistake to settle for someone who can be easily dominated as Leo bores quickly and actually expects their consort to give as good as they get. This contradiction aside, Leo is by nature a warm, loving and committed partner – occasionally even a cuddly cat – once they've found someone who can inspire them; enjoy and tolerate their slightly excessive natures; and keep up with their highly creative energy.

The Leo woman

If the Leo man is king, then the Leo woman embodies all the queenly virtues. She is romantic, intense, uninhibited and knows her rightful place is on a pedestal. This, combined with a very direct approach, can make her seem quite bold and a tad imperious, but dig a little deeper for her softer side with some truly meant compliments and attention and she'll retract her claws.

NOTABLE LEO WOMEN

Independent and determined, there's no messing with Madonna, who quite literally runs her own show, as does reality star and cosmetic-company founder Kylie Jenner, while successful actress Meghan Markle literally now has royal status as a member of the UK's first family. Famous courtesan and queen of Louis XV's mistresses Madame du Barry was Leo, as is queen of literature JK Rowling, and queen of JFK's Camelot, Jacqueline Kennedy Onassis.

The Leo man

A natural flirt with an appreciative eye, the Leo man can sometimes be so busy putting on a performance, he hardly notices when someone is giving him the eye. A bit like the lion, he's likely to enjoy the pursuit and when he's interested, it's easy to tell as he turns the full beam of his attention towards his goal.

Singers Joe Jonas and Shawn Mendes have all the charisma you'd expect from Leo, and both know how to play to big audiences and manage a crowd in a way that fellow Leo and celebrated Rolling Stone Mick Jagger did in his day. Other Leos include Barack Obama, whose direct gaze and charisma are also evident in actor Robert Redford and basketball star Magic Johnson.

Who love

s whom?

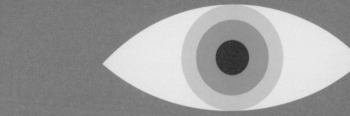

Leo & Aries

These two fire signs are often considered a match made in heaven, apart from one thing: their equally large egos. However, if they can use their natural rapport to overcome this in the bedroom and elsewhere, it's a very happy union.

Leo & Taurus

This coupling can be troubled by an immediate clash between Leo's flamboyance and Taurus' natural caution, after which the bull's stubbornness in their attempt to bring the lion down to earth may end in tears for both. Too tricky for many.

Leo & Gemini

Independence, *joie de vivre* and glamour mark this pairing with a sense of fun, which may be difficult to transfer from the bedroom to the real world. But if airy Gemini can make a commitment to Leo's demanding ways, it can work well.

Leo & Cancer

Romance dominates this
relationship and it can be
harmonious with Leo's need
for adoration well met by
Cancer's loyalty and intensity.
But Leo needs to be mindful
that a desire for public
acknowledgement makes
Cancer insecure.

Leo & Leo

If they can overcome the natural
inclination toward rivalry that
comes from two big egos, this
can be a very exciting and
intense affair, but they need
to work out who is in charge,
or take it in turns, otherwise the
passion could burn itself out.

Leo & Virgo

An unlikely fit, because the cool
intelligence of Virgo and refusal to
get excited about speculative plans
can dampen Leo's exuberant nature,
while Virgo's finesse and attention
to detail bewilders Leo, who is all
about the big picture.

Leo & Libra

Both share a love of beautiful things and that aesthetic appreciation gives them a lot in common. Plus, Leo's dominance doesn't irritate Libra, who rather likes someone else to make the decisions, both in and out of the bedroom.

Leo & Scorpio

There can be a bit of a stand-off here, between Leo's carefree, outgoing attitude and Scorpio's inclination to be rather intense and secretive. That clash in basic temperament isn't easy for either one to understand, or to placate.

Leo & Sagittarius

Similarly given to freedom and adventure, these two recognise an optimism and expansiveness in each that unites and excites them, including in the bedroom, where their fiery natures keep the passion going long after first meeting.

Leo & Aquarius

Despite an initial attraction that may get them into bed, Leo needs a lover who at least feigns devotion. Aquarius' airy indifference leaves them feeling bemused and, in the end, rejected. Leo just needs to be needed and Aquarius doesn't.

Leo & Pisces

Leo struggles with Pisces' mystical side which is so completely at odds with their need to be socialising on a public stage. Without a compromise, Leo's extroversion tends to clash with Pisces' need for a more contemplative life.

Leo & Capricorn

It's not an easy union between Leo's glamorous take on life and Capricorn's rather practical approach, making the latter seem rather disapproving to the former. And given their basic positions, there's little compromise either.

Leo love-o-meter

Least compatible

Taurus Virgo Scorpio Capricorn Pisces Aquarius

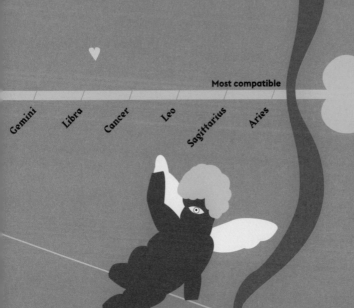

Most compatible

Gemini　　Libra　　Cancer　　Leo　　Sagittarius　　Aries

The

Leo

II.

Deep Dive

In this section, dive deeper into the ways in which your Sun sign might be driving you or holding you back, and start to think about how you might use this knowledge to inform your path.

The
Leo
home

Leo's home is their castle, quite literally in some cases. They have a penchant for grandeur and will make their home as luxurious as they can afford – if that includes gold taps in the bathroom, so much the better. Cool minimalism is unlikely to be a default position for Leo and there's something quite masculine and bold about their taste in interiors, with lots of vibrant colours and sumptuous fabrics, large paintings on the walls, and big coffee-table art books. Everything about Leo's home is likely to say bold and beautiful rather than shy and retiring. Ideally, the Palace at Versailles is optimum Leo style.

How this is tempered in more ordinary settings depends on the Leo concerned, but there are snatches of gold likely to be seen in picture frames, gilt candlesticks, gold satin cushion covers or in splashes of deep orange and citron in fabrics and furnishings. There may even be fur or quality faux fur rugs and in the colder months, a roaring open fire. What Leo wants to convey is that this is their kingdom and you are being welcomed into it.

TOP TIPS FOR
LEO SELF-CARE

★ Pace yourself, don't over-
   commit and ensure some
   me-time.

★ Regular, nutritious meals
   will fuel that Leo energy.

★ Alternate that high-octane
   work-out with a meditative
   swim to cool that Leo fire.

Self-care

Thinking twice before saying yes to every invite would be
a good start to self-care for Leo. Their naturally energetic
approach to life can mean that they take on too much, over-
committing themselves to work and social events only to then
wonder why they run out of steam. It's not so much fear of
missing out that keeps the pace high, but sheer enthusiasm and
the anticipation that everything is to be enjoyed and savoured.

Along with over-committing themselves, over-indulgence
is another tendency for Leo and when it comes to food and
drink, inevitably this can stack up with inches on the waistline
or hangovers in the morning. One smart move Leo could make
is to take up cooking their own meals, so at least what they eat
is nutritious. Cooking could also be a therapeutic use of time,
slowing them down and focusing on a creative activity that
can have a social side.

Regular exercise of a calming nature is also good for
hyperactive Leo. Not a high-octane workout that increases the
adrenaline drive, but something more relaxing which supports
both physical and mental health. Once the benefits of, say,
a twice-weekly Pilates class kick in and they see its value,
Leo can become as committed to that as to anything else.

WHAT TO KEEP IN THE LEO PANTRY

★ Golden Spanish saffron coupe grade.

★ Tins of caviar, or 'black gold'.

★ Traditional, aged balsamic vinegar of Modena.

Food
and
cooking

Leo likes to be a king in the kitchen as well as anywhere else, so cooking can become quite the event, and a sous chef is always welcome as an accomplice, audience and general assistant. Leo won't be cooking sausages and mash or a simple boiled egg – for them a meal is as much a performance as a production of *Carmen*, with as many exotic and expensive ingredients as can be included in a majestic beef wellington. What's more, this won't be a gentle *déjeuner pour deux* but the main course of a dinner party for 20, preceded by consommé and followed by home-made profiteroles. Oh, and a cheese course to go with the vintage port. Get the picture? Nothing is likely to be simple but everything will be executed with confidence and bravado; and will be both delicious and fit for a king.

TOP TIPS FOR LEO'S MONEY

★ Take a gamble but take advice first.

★ Curb impulse buying, even if it is a state-of-the-art lemon squeezer.

★ Be generous, but not profligate.

How
Leo
handles
money

Whoever said, 'we always regret our economies, but seldom our extravagances' was probably a Leo, renowned for their love of luxury. Impulse buys are another characteristic for a sign that tends to live for today and worry about tomorrow, tomorrow. And generally treats are of the more expensive kind, too – not just for themselves, but for others, because Leo can be a very generous gift giver. As might be imagined, though, saving for a rainy day doesn't feature much on their agenda, because for Leo the sun's always shining. Generally, they are lucky with money, and tend to earn it easily because of their natural enthusiasm for, and dedication to, work. When it comes to investments and a retirement plan, there is often interest in commodities like gold or fine wine and art; luxury items that mature over time, rather than stocks and shares or bricks and mortar. When it comes to financial planning, Leo can be quite creative about their strategy and it usually pays off.

How Leo handles the boss

Leo loves to work so is usually a welcome employee: energetic, good-natured, and – once they've got their teeth into a task – are well able to see it through. For a low-key type of boss, however, Leo may have to tone it down, pressing pause on their enthusiasm occasionally to listen without interruption. They may think they know best, but Leo shouldn't let their irritation at what they see as petty rules get in the way.

Leo can also be a perfectionist, so they struggle with co-workers who don't work to their standards, and often have no hesitation in pointing out other's inadequacies. Teamwork in general is a bit of a challenge for Leo, which can make difficulties for their boss, so this takes some careful handling all round.

Leo often changes jobs, sometimes through promotion, but also because they change careers in an effort to find work stimulating. They're 100 per cent committed while they're there, but they may not be there for longer than it takes them to reach the next rung on the ladder of their career.

TOP TIPS TO HANDLE THE BOSS

★ More haste, less speed usually yields better results.

★ Remember that you *have* a boss, and check in with them at least occasionally.

★ Give credit to teammates where credit is due.

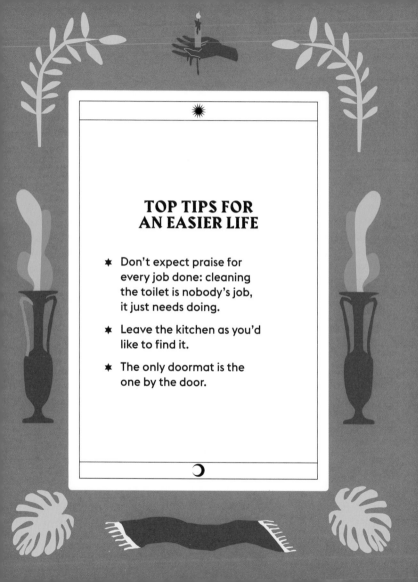

TOP TIPS FOR
AN EASIER LIFE

★ Don't expect praise for
every job done: cleaning
the toilet is nobody's job,
it just needs doing.

★ Leave the kitchen as you'd
like to find it.

★ The only doormat is the
one by the door.

What is Leo like to live with?

Never a dull moment, living with Leo, except when they're asleep. In theory, once you get the hang of them, this good-natured sign is easy to be around, as not much seems to bother them. But it might bother their flatmates when they endlessly leave towels on the bathroom floor or the washing up stacked next to the sink as they rush out on yet another big adventure ... or perhaps just because they are late for work.

Rotas for chores don't really work for Leo, because the king of the jungle probably has other things on their mind and such domestic minutiae can be of little consequence. However, the contradiction is that Leo actually wants to live in lovely surroundings so isn't by nature slovenly, it's just that they would prefer someone else to do the domestic donkey-work as, frankly, they probably think it's a little beneath them. If a housemate suggests hiring a cleaner, you can bet they're a Leo.

If there are any difficulties between you, Leo will let you know, but they seldom hold a grudge; their roar is much worse than their bite and quarrels are quickly forgotten.

How to handle a break-up

There's no way a break-up will be without drama, but a lion in pain tends to roar, whether they've got a splinter in their paw or a life-threatening wound. Another Leo reaction to a break-up is to ignore it: pretend they're absolutely fine and didn't care anyway, even though inside that heart can be badly wounded. Whether they're roaring or quietly seething, they often try to show the world they don't care by throwing themselves into extravagant, exhausting socialising. The good thing about Leo is that their bruised heart recovers quickly, and it won't be long before they're back dating. In their magnanimous way, Leo tends to expect to be friends with their exes further down the line.

TOP TIPS FOR AN EASIER BREAK-UP

★ Don't make a performance out of it: being 'tired and emotional' seldom helps.

★ Confide in a few close friends.

★ Allow some time before trying to be friends with an ex.

How Leo wants to be loved

Put simply, adoringly and unconditionally is what Leo wants when it comes to being loved. At first glance, this looks very simple but they are more complicated than they look and also one of the proudest signs of the zodiac, which can make them vulnerable. In fact, Leo's apparent need for unconditional adoration, and their reaction when they don't get it, can come from a deep insecurity in spite of all the outgoing brashness. So for all their obvious desire for attention and appreciation, the irony is that this can sometimes be rooted in a need for validation. The fact that Leo finds lack of self-esteem and feelings of insecurity in others unattractive is a bit of a clue, as they may struggle with this occasionally themselves.

Because of this paradox, loving Leo can be a bit of a challenge, and it takes a lot longer than it might first appear to get them to commit, partly because they need to be sure, but also because they need to be sure of themselves. If Leo has a bit of a reputation as being commitment-phobic, flitting from one relationship to another or having more than one on the go at the same time, this can sometimes come from an inability to fully trust that they are lovable. And because they seem so self-confident, this aspect of the lion sometimes gets covered up in a don't-care attitude. Sometimes it takes a bit of grounded patience to get through these self-imposed barriers that proud Leo puts up, but it's not for want of loving feelings, which they have in abundance and are happy to reciprocate, once they feel really secure.

Leo is also about having fun, fun, fun; so this welcomes handling with a light touch. Not given to huge introspection like some of the watery zodiac signs, Leo will respond well to dates that involve straightforward activities: whether it's a luxury dinner, funny movie at the cinema, playing Twister or charades – Leo have a child-like appreciation for fun. Doing things together and creating relationships based on mutually shared interests and activities – like a love of rock climbing or salsa dancing – can be a great way of loving Leo. Given all this, Leo partners aren't for the faint hearted, but behind that ego is a loving, caring, loyal lover – remember, many lions mate for life so they sometimes take their time playing the field first.

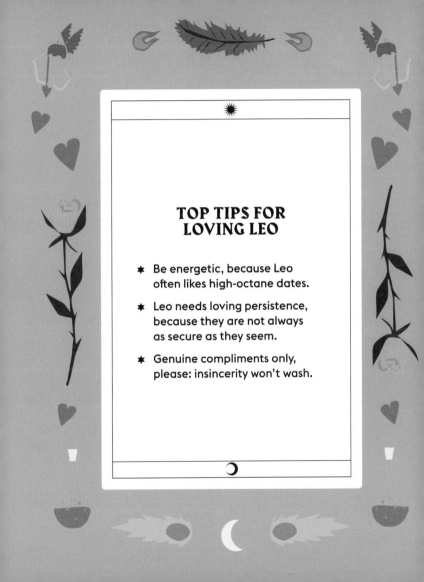

TOP TIPS FOR LOVING LEO

* Be energetic, because Leo often likes high-octane dates.

* Leo needs loving persistence, because they are not always as secure as they seem.

* Genuine compliments only, please: insincerity won't wash.

Leo's sex life

For a sensuous sign like Leo, sex is a pleasure to make them purr and sometimes roar and no better place to start than with their back. For Leo, in particular, this is an erogenous area, and massaging the full length of the spine to the buttocks is a wonderful start. There's definitely a sense of performance but there's also a generosity because Leo likes to give as much as to receive in the bedroom: it's all part of their regal beneficence. A part of Leo's sensuality is to look, so a full black-out is unlikely – and they also enjoy hearing how good it all is, not only when talking dirty but also in praise afterwards. All in all, making love is a very inclusive business for Leo, and their focus is definitely on sharing a great experience.

Leo may be sexy but they also understand the importance of romance. So the lighting may be in candle form, and the foreplay is seldom skimped. This is also an adventurous sign that isn't above a little risk taking, so *en plein air* sex may be on the cards, or sex in unexpected places and certainly not limited to the bedroom. It's often fun too, for Leo, who is quite capable of laughing their partners into bed before anyone realises quite how serious it's getting.

Give
III.

Me & More

Your Sun sign never shows you the whole picture. In this section, learn how to read the nuances of your birth chart and discover a whole new level of astrological insight.

Your birth chart

Your birth chart is a snapshot of a particular moment, in a particular place, at the precise moment of your birth and is therefore completely individual to you. It's like a blueprint, a map, a statement of occurrence, spelling out possible traits and influences – but it isn't your destiny. It is just a symbolic tool to which you can refer, based on the position of the planets at the time of your birth. If you can't get to an astrologer, these days anyone can get their birth chart prepared in minutes online (see page 108 for a list of websites and apps that will do it for you). Even if you don't know your exact time of birth, just knowing the date and place of birth can create the beginnings of a useful template.

Remember, nothing is intrinsically good or bad in astrology and there is no explicit timing or forecasting: it's more a question of influences and how these might play out positively or negatively. And if we have some insight, and some tools with which to approach, see or interpret our circumstances and surroundings, this gives us something to work with.

When you are reading your birth chart, it's useful to first understand all the tools of astrology available to you; not only the astrological signs and what they represent, but also the 10 planets referred to in astrology and their individual characteristics, along with the 12 houses and what they mean. Individually, these tools of astrology are of passing interest, but when you start to see how they might sit in juxtaposition to each other, then the bigger picture becomes more accessible and we begin to gain insights that can be useful to us.

Broadly speaking, each of the planets suggests a different type of energy, the astrological signs propose the various ways in which that energy might be expressed, while the houses represent areas of experience in which this expression might operate.

Next to bring into the picture are the positions of the signs at four key points: the ascendant, or rising sign, and its opposite, the descendant; and the midheaven and its opposite, the IC, not to mention the different aspects created by congregations of signs and planets.

It is now possible to see how subtle the reading of a birth chart might be and how it is infinite in its variety, and highly specific to an individual. With this information, and a working understanding of the symbolic meaning and influences of the signs, planets and houses of your unique astrological profile, you can begin to use these tools to help with decision-making and other aspects of life.

Reading your chart

If you have your birth chart prepared, either by hand or via an online program, you will see a circle divided into 12 segments, with information clustered at various points indicating the position of each zodiac sign, in which segment it appears and at what degree. Irrespective of the features that are relevant to the individual, each chart follows the same pattern when it comes to interpretation.

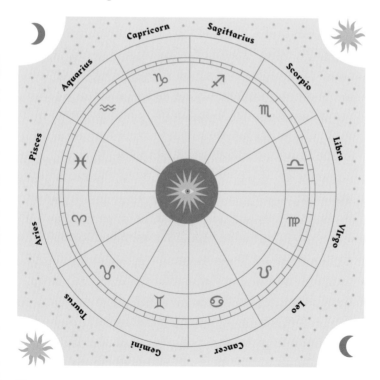

Given the time of birth, the place of birth and the position of the planets at that moment, the birth chart, sometimes called a natal horoscope, is drawn up.

If you consider the chart as a clock face, the first house (see pages 95–99 for the astrological houses) begins at the 9, and it is from this point that, travelling anti-clockwise the chart is read from the first house, through the 12 segments of the chart to the twelfth.

The beginning point, the 9, is also the point at which the Sun rises on your life, giving you your ascendant, or rising sign, and opposite to this, at the 3 of the clock face, is your descendant sign. The midheaven point of your chart, the MC, is at 12, and its opposite, the IC, at 6 (see pages 101–102).

Understanding the significance of the characteristics of the astrological signs and the planets, their particular energies, their placements and their aspects to each other can be helpful in understanding ourselves and our relationships with others. In day-to-day life, too, the changing configuration of planets and their effects are much more easily understood with a basic knowledge of astrology, as are the recurring patterns that can sometimes strengthen and sometimes delay opportunities and possibilities. Working with, rather than against, these trends can make life more manageable and, in the last resort, more successful.

The
Moon
effect

If your Sun sign represents your consciousness, your life force and your individual will, then the Moon represents that side of your personality that you tend to keep rather secret or hidden. This is the realm of instinct, intuition, creativity and the unconscious, which can take you places emotionally that are sometimes hard to understand. This is what brings great subtlety and nuance to a person, way beyond just their Sun sign. So you may have your Sun in Leo, and all that means, but this might be countered by a strongly empathetic and feeling Moon in Cancer; or you may have your Sun in loyal, earthy Taurus, but a Moon in Aquarius with all its rebellious, emotional detachment.

Phases of the Moon

The Moon orbits the Earth, taking roughly 28 days to do so. How much of the Moon we see is determined by how much of the Sun's light it reflects, giving us the impression that it waxes, or grows, and wanes. When the Moon is new, to us, only a sliver of it is illuminated. As it waxes, it reflects more light and moves from a crescent, to a waxing crescent to a first quarter; then it moves to a waxing gibbous Moon, to a full Moon. Then the Moon begins to wane through a waning gibbous, to a last quarter, and then the cycle begins again. All of this occurs over four weeks. When we have two full Moons in any one calendar month, the second is called a blue Moon.

Each month the Moon also moves through an astrological sign, as we know from our personal birth charts. This, too, will yield information – a Moon in Scorpio can have a very different effect to one in Capricorn – and depending on our personal charts, this can have a shifting influence each month. For example, if the Moon in your birth chart is in Virgo, then when the actual Moon moves into Virgo, this will have an additional influence. Read the characteristics of the signs for further information (see pages 12–17).

The Moon's cycle has an energetic effect, which we can see quite easily on the ocean tides. Astrologically, because the Moon is both a fertility symbol and attuned to our deeper psychological side, we can use this to focus more profoundly and creatively on aspects of life that are important to us.

Eclipses

Generally speaking, an eclipse covers up and prevents light being shed on a situation. Astrologically speaking, this will depend on where the Sun or Moon is positioned in relation to other planets at the time of an eclipse. So if a solar eclipse is in Gemini, there will be a Geminian influence or an influence on Geminis.

Hiding, or shedding, light on an area of our lives is an invitation to pay attention to it. Eclipses are generally about beginnings or endings, which is why our ancestors saw them as portents, important signs to be taken notice of. As it is possible to know when an eclipse is forthcoming, these are charted astronomically; consequently, their astrological significance can be assessed and acted upon ahead of time.

The 10 planets

For the purpose of astrology (but not for astronomy, because the Sun is really a star) we talk about 10 planets, and each astrological sign has a ruling planet, with Mercury, Venus and Mars each being assigned two. The characteristics of each planet describe those influences that can affect signs, all of which information feeds into the interpretation of a birth chart.

The Moon

This sign is an opposing principle to the Sun, forming a pair, and it represents the feminine, symbolising containment and receptivity, how we react most instinctively and with feeling.

Rules the sign of Cancer.

The Sun

The Sun represents the masculine, and is seen as the energy that sparks life, which suggests a paternal energy in our birth chart. It also symbolises our self or essential being, and our purpose.

Rules the sign of Leo.

Mercury

Mercury is the planet of communication and symbolises our urge to make sense of, understand and communicate our thoughts through words.

Rules the signs of Gemini and Virgo.

Venus

The planet of love is all about attraction, connection and pleasure and in a female chart it symbolises her style of femininity, while in a male chart it represents his ideal partner.

Rules the signs of Taurus and Libra.

Mars

This planet symbolises pure energy (Mars was, after all, the god of War) but it also tells you in which areas you're most likely to be assertive, aggressive or to take risks.

Rules the signs of Aries and Scorpio.

Saturn

Saturn is sometimes called the wise
teacher or taskmaster of astrology,
symbolising lessons learnt and
limitations, showing us the value of
determination, tenacity and resilience.

Rules the sign of Capricorn.

Jupiter

The planet Jupiter is the largest in our
solar system and symbolises bounty
and benevolence, all that is expansive
and jovial. Like the sign it rules, it's
also about moving away from the
home on journeys and exploration.

Rules the sign of Sagittarius.

Uranus

This planet symbolises
the unexpected, new ideas and
innovation, and the urge to tear down
the old and usher in the new. The
downside can mark an inability to fit
in and consequently the feeling
of being an outsider.

Rules the sign of Aquarius.

Pluto

Aligned to Hades (*Pluto* in Latin), the god of the underworld or death, the planet exerts a powerful force that lies below the surface and which, in its most negative form, can represent obsessions and compulsive behaviour.

Rules the sign of Scorpio.

Neptune

Linked to the sea, this is about what lies beneath, underwater and too deep to be seen clearly. Sensitive, intuitive and artistic, it also symbolises the capacity to love unconditionally, to forgive and forget.

Rules the sign of Pisces.

The four elements

Further divisions of the 12 astrological signs into the four elements of earth, fire, air and water yield other characteristics. This comes from ancient Greek medicine, where the body was considered to be made up of four bodily fluids or 'humours'. These four humours – blood, yellow bile, black bile and phlegm – corresponded to the four temperaments of sanguine, choleric, melancholic and phlegmatic, to the four seasons of the year, spring, summer, autumn, winter, and the four elements of air, fire, earth and water.

Related to astrology, these symbolic qualities cast further light on characteristics of the different signs. Carl Jung also used them in his psychology, and we still refer to people as earthy, fiery, airy or wet in their approach to life, while sometimes describing people as 'being in their element'. In astrology, those Sun signs that share the same element are said to have an affinity, or an understanding, with each other.

Like all aspects of astrology, there is always a positive and a negative, and a knowledge of any 'shadow side' can be helpful in terms of self-knowledge and what we may need to enhance or balance out, particularly in our dealings with others.

Air

GEMINI ✳ LIBRA ✳ AQUARIUS

Fire

ARIES ✳ LEO ✳ SAGITTARIUS

The realm of ideas is where these air signs excel. Perceptive and visionary and able to see the big picture, there is a very reflective quality to air signs that helps to vent situations. Too much air, however, can dissipate intentions, so Gemini might be indecisive, Libra has a tendency to sit on the fence, while Aquarius can be very disengaged.

There is a warmth and energy to these signs, a positive approach, spontaneity and enthusiasm that can be inspiring and very motivational to others. The downside is that Aries has a tendency to rush in headfirst, Leo can have a need for attention and Sagittarius can tend to talk it up but not deliver.

Earth

TAURUS ✳ VIRGO ✳ CAPRICORN

Characteristically, these
signs enjoy sensual pleasure,
enjoying food and other
physical pleasures, and
they like to feel grounded,
preferring to base their ideas
in facts. The downside is that
Taureans can be stubborn,
Virgos can be pernickety and
Capricorns can veer towards
a dogged conservatism.

Water

CANCER ✳ SCORPIO ✳ PISCES

Water signs are very
responsive, like the tide
ebbing and flowing, and
can be very perceptive
and intuitive, sometimes
uncannily so because of their
ability to feel. The downside
is – watery enough – a
tendency to feel swamped,
and then Cancer can be both
tenacious and self-protective,
Pisces chameleon-like in
their attention and Scorpio
unpredictable and intense.

Cardinal, fixed and mutable signs

In addition to the 12 signs being divided into four elements, they can also be grouped into three different ways in which their energies may act or react, giving further depth to each sign's particular characteristics.

Cardinal

ARIES ✳ CANCER ✳ LIBRA ✳ CAPRICORN

These are action planets, with an energy that takes the initiative and gets things started. Aries has the vision, Cancer the feelings, Libra the contacts and Capricorn the strategy.

Fixed

TAURUS ✷ LEO ✷ SCORPIO ✷ AQUARIUS

Slower but more determined, these signs work to progress and maintain those initiatives that the cardinal signs have fired up. Taurus offers physical comfort, Leo loyalty, Scorpio emotional support and Aquarius sound advice. You can count on fixed signs, but they tend to resist change.

Mutable

GEMINI ✷ VIRGO ✷ SAGITTARIUS ✷ PISCES

Adaptable and responsive to new ideas, places and people, mutable signs have a unique ability to adjust to their surroundings. Gemini is mentally agile, Virgo is practical and versatile, Sagittarius visualises possibilities and Pisces is responsive to change.

The 12 houses

The birth chart is divided into 12 houses, which represent separate areas and functions of your life. When you are told you have something in a specific house – for example, Libra (balance) in the fifth house (creativity and sex) – it creates a way of interpreting the influences that can arise and are particular to how you might approach an aspect of your life.

Each house relates to a Sun sign, and in this way each is represented by some of the characteristics of that sign, which is said to be its natural ruler.

Three of these houses are considered to be mystical, relating to our interior, psychic world: the fourth (home), eighth (death and regeneration) and twelfth (secrets).

1st House

THE SELF

RULED BY ARIES

This house symbolises the self: you, who you are and how you represent yourself, your likes, dislikes and approach to life. It also represents how you see yourself and what you want in life.

2nd House

POSSESSIONS

RULED BY TAURUS

The second house symbolises your possessions, what you own, including money; how you earn or acquire your income; and your material security and the physical things you take with you as you move through life.

3rd House

COMMUNICATION

RULED BY GEMINI

This house is about communication and mental attitude, primarily how you express yourself. It's also about how you function within your family, and how you travel to school or work, and includes how you think, speak, write and learn.

4th House

HOME

RULED BY CANCER

This house is about your roots and your home or homes, present, past and future, so it includes both your childhood and current domestic set-up. It's also about what home and security represent to you.

5th House

CREATIVITY

RULED BY LEO

Billed as the house of creativity and play, this also includes sex, and relates to the creative urge, the libido, in all its manifestations. It's also about speculation in finance and love, games, fun and affection: affairs of the heart.

6th House

HEALTH

RULED BY VIRGO

This house is related to health: our own physical and emotional health, and how robust it is; but also those we care for, look after or provide support to – from family members to work colleagues.

7th House

PARTNERSHIPS

RULED BY LIBRA

The opposite of the first house, this reflects shared goals and intimate partnerships, our choice of life partner and how successful our relationships might be. It also reflects partnerships and adversaries in our professional world.

8th House

REGENERATION

RULED BY SCORPIO

For death, read regeneration or spiritual transformation: this house also reflects legacies and what you inherit after death, in personality traits or materially. And because regeneration requires sex, it's also about sex and sexual emotions.

9th House

TRAVEL

RULED BY SAGITTARIUS

The house of long-distance travel and exploration, this is also about the broadening of the mind that travel can bring, and how that might express itself. It also reflects the sending out of ideas, which can come about from literary effort or publication.

11th House

FRIENDSHIPS

RULED BY AQUARIUS

The eleventh house is about friendship groups and acquaintances, vision and ideas, and is less about immediate gratification but more concerning longer-term dreams and how these might be realised through our ability to work harmoniously with others.

12th House

SECRETS

RULED BY PISCES

Considered the most spiritual house, it is also the house of the unconscious, of secrets and of what might lie hidden, the metaphorical skeleton in the closet. It also reflects the secret ways we might self-sabotage or imprison our own efforts by not exploring them.

10th House

ASPIRATIONS

RULED BY CAPRICORN

This represents our aspiration and status, how we'd like to be elevated in public standing (or not), our ambitions, image and what we'd like to attain in life, through our own efforts.

The ascendant

Otherwise known as your rising sign, this is the sign of the zodiac that appears at the horizon as dawn breaks on the day of your birth, depending on your location in the world and time of birth. This is why knowing your time of birth is a useful factor in astrology, because your 'rising sign' yields a lot of information about those aspects of your character that are more on show, how you present yourself and how you are seen by others. So, even if you are a Sun Leo, but have Cancer rising, you may be seen as someone who is maternal, with a noticeable commitment to the domestic life in one way or another. Knowing your own ascendant – or that of another person – will often help explain why there doesn't seem to be such a direct correlation between their personality and their Sun sign.

As long as you know your time of birth and where you were born, working out your ascendant using an online tool or app is very easy (see page 108). Just ask your mum or other family members, or check your birth certificate (in those countries that include a birth time). If the astrological chart were a clock face, the ascendant would be at the 9 o'clock position.

The descendant

The descendant gives an indication of a possible life partner, based on the idea that opposites attract. Once you know your ascendant, the descendant is easy to work out as it is always six signs away: for example, if your ascendant is Virgo, your descendant is Pisces. If the astrological chart were a clock face, the descendant would be at the 3 o'clock position.

The midheaven (MC)

Also included in the birth chart is the position of the midheaven or MC (from the Latin, *medium coeli,* meaning middle of the heavens), which indicates your attitude towards your work, career and professional standing. If the astrological chart were a clock face, the MC would be at the 12 o'clock position.

The IC

Finally, your IC (from the Latin, *imum coeli,* meaning the lowest part of the heavens) indicates your attitude towards your home and family, and is also related to the end of your life. Your IC will be directly opposite your MC: for example, if your MC is Aquarius, your IC is Leo. If the astrological chart were a clock face, the IC would be at the 6 o'clock position.

Saturn return

Saturn is one of the slower-moving planets, taking around 28 years to complete its orbit around the Sun and return to the place it occupied at the time of your birth. This return can last between two to three years and be very noticeable in the period coming up to our thirtieth and sixtieth birthdays, often considered to be significant 'milestone' birthdays.

Because the energy of Saturn is sometimes experienced as demanding, this isn't always an easy period of life. A wise teacher or a hard taskmaster, some consider the Saturn effect as 'cruel to be kind' in the way that many good teachers can be, keeping us on track like a rigorous personal trainer.

Everyone experiences their Saturn return relevant to their circumstances, but it is a good time to take stock, let go of the stuff in your life that no longer serves you and revise your expectations, while being unapologetic about what you would like to include more of in your life. So if you are experiencing or anticipating this life event, embrace and work with it because what you learn now – about yourself, mainly – is worth knowing, however turbulent it might be, and can pay dividends in how you manage the next 28 years!

Mercury retrograde

Even those with little interest in astrology often take notice when the planet Mercury is retrograde. Astrologically, retrogrades are periods when planets are stationary but, as we continue to move forwards, Mercury 'appears' to move backwards. There is a shadow period either side of a retrograde period, when it could be said to be slowing down or speeding up, which can also be a little turbulent. Generally speaking, the advice is not to make any important moves related to communication on a retrograde and, even if a decision is made, know that it's likely to change.

Given that Mercury is the planet of communication, you can immediately see why there are concerns about its retrograde status and its link to communication failures – of the old-fashioned sort when the post office loses a letter, or the more modern technological variety when your computer crashes

– causing problems. Mercury retrograde can also affect travel, with delays in flights or train times, traffic jams or collisions. Mercury also influences personal communications: listening, speaking, being heard (or not), and can cause confusion or arguments. It can also affect more formal agreements, like contracts between buyer and seller.

These retrograde periods occur three to four times a year, lasting for roughly three weeks, with a shadow period either side. The dates in which it happens also mean it occurs within a specific astrological sign. If, for example, it occurs between 25 October and 15 November, its effect would be linked to the characteristics of Scorpio. In addition, those Sun sign Scorpios, or those with Scorpio in significant placements in their chart, may also experience a greater effect.

Mercury retrograde dates are easy to find from an astrological table, or ephemeris, and online. These can be used in order to avoid planning events that might be affected around these times. How Mercury retrograde may affect you more personally requires knowledge of your birth chart and an understanding of its more specific combination of influences with the signs and planets in your chart.

If you are going to weather a Mercury retrograde more easily, be aware that glitches can occur so, to some extent, expect delays and double-check details. Stay positive if postponements occur and consider this period an opportunity to slow down, review or reconsider ideas in your business or your personal life. Use the time to correct mistakes or reshape plans, preparing for when any stuck energy can shift and you can move forward again more smoothly.

Further reading

Astrology Decoded (2013) by Sue Merlyn Farebrother; published by Rider

Astrology for Dummies (2007) by Rae Orion; published by Wiley Publishing

Chart Interpretation Handbook: Guidelines for Understanding the Essentials of the Birth Chart (1990) by Stephen Arroyo; published by CRCS Publications

Jung's Studies in Astrology (2018) by Liz Greene; published by RKP

The Only Astrology Book You'll Ever Need (2012) by Joanne Woolfolk; published by Taylor Trade

Websites

astro.com

astrologyzone.com

jessicaadams.com

shelleyvonstrunkel.com

Apps

Astrostyle

Co-Star

Susan Miller's Astrology Zone

The Daily Horoscope

The Pattern

Time Passages

Acknowledgements

Particular thanks are due to my trusty team of Taureans. Firstly, to Kate Pollard, Publishing Director at Hardie Grant, for her passion for beautiful books and for commissioning this series. And to Bex Fitzsimons for all her good natured and conscientious editing. And finally to Evi O. Studio, whose illustration and design talents have produced small works of art. With such a star-studded team, these books can only shine and for that, my thanks.

About the author

Stella Andromeda has been studying astrology for over 30 years, believing that a knowledge of the constellations of the skies and their potential for psychological interpretation can be a useful tool. This extension of her study into book form makes modern insights about the ancient wisdom of the stars easily accessible, sharing her passion that reflection and self-knowledge only empowers us in life. With her sun in Taurus, Aquarius ascendant and Moon in Cancer, she utilises earth, air and water to inspire her own astrological journey.

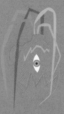

Published in 2019 by Hardie Grant Books,
an imprint of Hardie Grant Publishing

Hardie Grant Books (London)
5th & 6th Floors
52–54 Southwark Street
London SE1 1UN

Hardie Grant Books (Melbourne)
Building 1, 658 Church Street
Richmond, Victoria 3121

hardiegrantbooks.com

British Library Cataloguing-in-Publication Data. A catalogue record
for this book is available from the British Library.

Leo
ISBN: 9781784882624

10 9 8 7 6 5

Publishing Director: Kate Pollard
Junior Editor: Bex Fitzsimons
Art Direction and Illustrations: Evi O. Studio
Editor: Wendy Hobson
Production Controller: Sinead Hering

Colour reproduction by p2d
Printed and bound in China by Leo Paper Products Ltd.